My First CHRiSTMAS Book

Jane
Winstanley

W

FRANKLIN WATTS

LONDON • SYDNEY

Franklin Watts
First published in Great Britain in 2015 by
The Watts Publishing Group

Credits

Editor: Nicola Barber
Design: Storeybooks
Picture Research: Diana Morris
Illustrator: Shelagh McNicholas, pp 6–9
Cover design: Cathyrn Gilbert
Extra artwork by Ruth Walton
Commissioned photography:
   Paul Bricknell Photography, pp10–11, 13, 16–17,
   21(bottom), 30, 32–3, 35
Tudor Photography, Banbury 12–13, 20–1, 22–3,
   26–9

Dewey number 745.5'9412
HB ISBN 978 1445 1 3826 8
Library ebook ISBN 978 1 4451 3877 0

Printed in China

MIX
Paper from
responsible sources
FSC www.fsc.org FSC® C104740

Franklin Watts
An imprint of Hachette Children's Group
Part of The Watts Publishing Group
Carmelite House
50 Victoria Embankment
London EC4Y 0DZ

An Hachette UK Company
www.hachette.co.uk

www.franklinwatts.co.uk

Picture credits:
Alias Ching/Shutterstock pp2, 3, 24bg; Sofi photo/
Shutterstock (gift card) pp4, 10, 12, 14, 16, 18, 20,
22, 24, 26, 28; Marcin Pawlinski/Dreamstime 4b;
Spencer Grant/Alamy 5tl; Paula Solloway/Alamy 5tr;
Sorge/Caro/Alamy 5bl; Jim Ringland/Art Directors/
Alamy 5br; Rosa Jay/Shutterstock 7; Julie A. Felton/
Shutterstock (lights) 14; Nalinn/Shutterstock 14tr;
Anteromite/Shutterstock 14br; Sandra Cunningham/
Shutterstock: 15tl; World of vector/Shutterstock 15c;
Judilyn/ Shutterstock 15tr; gift tag 15b; Kalenik
Hanna/Shutterstock 18, 19bg; Mountainpix/
Shutterstock 18c; Yakobina/Shutterstock 18b;
Wikimedia Commons 19t; Andere/Shutterstock 19c;
Joingate/Shutterstock 19b; Ratselmeister/Shutterstock
23; Cubo Images/Superstock 24b; Madeleine
Openshaw/Shutterstock 25t; Iakov Filimonov /
Shutterstock 25b; National Archives, London/Mary
Evans PL 27.

Contents

What is Christmas?

Christmas Day is on 25 December. It is celebrated by people all over the world.

Midwinter celebrations

Long before anyone had heard of Christmas, people held winter celebrations. In England, there was a **midwinter** festival on the shortest day of the year. In the cold, dark days of winter it reminded everyone that the warm, light days would be back again in spring.

Celebrating the birth of Jesus

Christmas celebrates the birth of the baby Jesus Christ. No one knows exactly when Jesus was born. The old midwinter festivals turned into a celebration of his birthday, called Christ's **Mass** – which became 'Christmas'.

How do you celebrate Christmas?

People celebrate Christmas in many different ways. These children are enjoying some Christmas activities. What's your favourite part of Christmas?

The Christmas story

Around 2,000 years ago, in a small town called Nazareth, there was a girl by the name of Mary. She was **engaged** to be married to a boy called Joseph.

One night, an angel appeared to Mary. The angel told her that God had chosen her to be the mother of his son on Earth. She must call the baby Jesus. Mary was frightened, but excited too.

An angel appeared to Joseph and told him the good news. Soon after the angel's visit, Mary and Joseph were married.

At that time the Romans ruled the land where Mary and Joseph lived. The Romans ordered everyone to return to the place they had been born.

They wanted to count people to make sure they paid their **taxes**. Mary and Joseph had to travel to Bethlehem, Joseph's home town.

It was a very long journey. They had only a donkey to carry them. When they reached Bethlehem, Mary knew it was time for the baby to be born.

Joseph looked for somewhere to stay. Everywhere was full. An innkeeper offered them a stable to sleep in. Sheep and cattle sheltered there, but it was warm and dry. Joseph made Mary as comfortable as he could.

That night, Mary gave birth to a baby boy. She wrapped him in **swaddling clothes** and placed him in a **manger**.

In a field outside Bethlehem, an angel appeared to some shepherds. The angel told the shepherds about the birth of baby Jesus. They were excited and went to find him.

A bright star appeared in the sky above Bethlehem. Three kings saw the star and set out to follow it. On the way they went to see King Herod. They told Herod about the star. They said a new king had been born. Herod pretended to be pleased – but he did not want a new king in his land. He asked the wise men to let him know where the baby king could be found.

The three kings followed the star to Bethlehem. They worshipped Jesus and gave him gifts of gold, **frankincense** and **myrrh**. But they did not tell Herod how to find the baby.

Herod was furious. In his rage, he ordered every boy in Bethlehem under the age of two to be killed.

An angel warned Joseph of the danger. He and Mary fled with the baby Jesus to Egypt. They stayed there until they heard news of Herod's death. Only then was it safe for them to return to Nazareth.

Make an Advent calendar

It is fun to make your own **Advent** calendar. Use some small pictures of family, friends, pets and pictures of favourite places.

You will need:
* 2 sheets of thin card (A3 size)
* matchbox and pencil
* craft knife
* glue and spatula
* 24 pictures to go inside the windows
* coloured felt-tipped pens

Instructions

1 On one sheet of card, draw round the matchbox 24 times.

2 Ask an adult to cut along the top and bottom lines of each rectangle with the craft knife. Then cut a line down the centre of each rectangle, from top to bottom (an H-shape on its side).

3 With the spatula, carefully spread glue around all the rectangles.

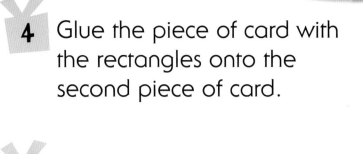

4 Glue the piece of card with the rectangles onto the second piece of card.

5 Carefully fold back the flaps of each rectangle to make windows. Glue a picture onto the backing card in each window. Then leave to dry.

6 Press the flaps back in place. Write the numbers 1 to 24 on the windows, then decorate your calendar.

What is Advent?

The time before Christmas is called Advent. Advent begins on the fourth Sunday before Christmas and lasts until Christmas Eve.

In some churches people light a red candle on each of the four Sundays in Advent, and a white one on Christmas Day to mark Jesus's birthday.

Advent calendars have a window to open each day from 1 December to Christmas Eve.

Make thumbprint Christmas cards

Turn your thumbprints into reindeer, robins, snowmen, trees and lots of other Christmassy things.

You will need:
* piece of card folded in half (to fit in an envelope if you want to post it)
* green poster paints
* plate
* scrap paper
* felt-tip pens

Instructions

1 Squeeze a blob of green paint onto the plate.

2 Dip your thumb in the green paint.

3 Try out some thumbprints on the scrap of paper to make sure you have not got too much paint on your thumb

4 Now make a triangle of green thumbprints on the card as shown in the picture on the right. Leave them to dry.

12

5 Use a brown felt-tip pen to draw a trunk. Use a red felt-tip pen to draw a star and decorations.

6 To make a reindeer card, use red paint to make two thumbprints. With the felt-tip pens draw a nose (red for Rudolf!), eyes, antlers, tail and legs.

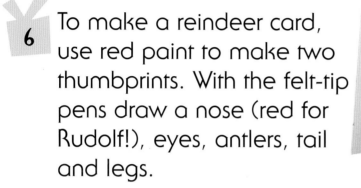

7 To make a robin card, use two red thumbprints. Draw on a beak, eye, wings and feet.

8 To create a snowman card, make two thumbprints for each snowman. Draw on a hat, buttons, nose, eyes, mouth and arms.

What other Christmassy things can you make from your thumbprint?

Put your card in an envelope and post it to a friend... Don't forget the stamp!

Cards and decorations

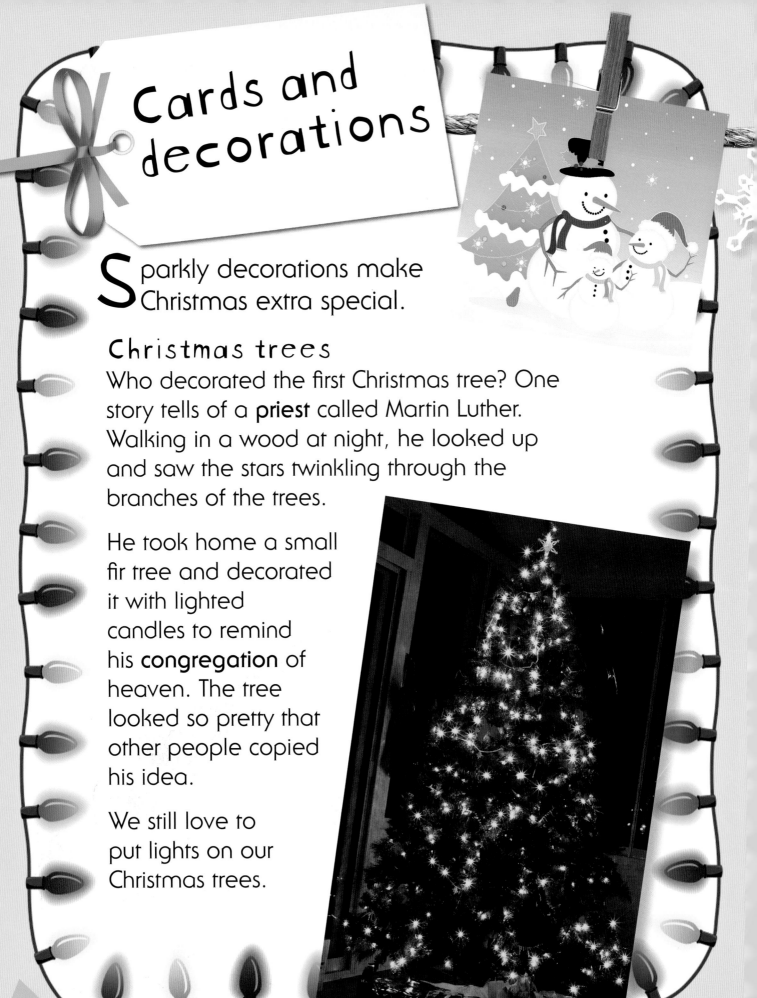

Sparkly decorations make Christmas extra special.

Christmas trees

Who decorated the first Christmas tree? One story tells of a **priest** called Martin Luther. Walking in a wood at night, he looked up and saw the stars twinkling through the branches of the trees.

He took home a small fir tree and decorated it with lighted candles to remind his **congregation** of heaven. The tree looked so pretty that other people copied his idea.

We still love to put lights on our Christmas trees.

Christmas cards

Lots of people send and receive Christmas cards each year. It is a great way to say 'Happy Christmas'.

The idea for the first Christmas card came from a man called Sir Henry Cole, in 1843. He sold around 2,000 Christmas cards that year.

By the 1870s, sending cards at Christmas was popular in England, and in the United States too.

Eco tip

Why not turn last year's cards into this year's gift tags?

Cut the picture on the card into the shape of the tag you want.

Make a hole with a hole punch.

Thread some string or ribbon through the hole.

Make an angel decoration

This easy-to-make angel decoration will look brilliant hanging on your Christmas tree.

Instructions

1 Starting at a short end, fold over 1cm of the paper. Turn the paper over and fold back 1cm. Keep doing this until you have a fan shape.

2 Tie the fan tightly together with the ribbon, 2cm from one end.

3 Open the fan out at both ends.

4 Cut a pair of wings out of the card. Glue them onto the back of the fan behind the ribbon.

5 Cut out a head shape. Draw on a face with the felt-tip pens. Glue the head to the top of the fan.

6 Glue a loop of ribbon to the back of the head.

Hang your angel on your Christmas tree.

Angels

Angels are an important part of the Christmas story.

An angel appeared to both Mary and Joseph to tell them about the baby Jesus. Another angel found the shepherds to tell them Jesus had been born. And it was an angel who warned the three kings not to tell King Herod where the baby Jesus lay.

All about Father Christmas

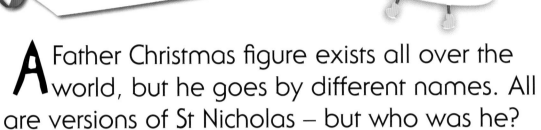

A Father Christmas figure exists all over the world, but he goes by different names. All are versions of St Nicholas – but who was he?

St Nicholas

St Nicholas was a Christian who spent his life looking after people who needed his help – particularly sailors and children.

Christmas stockings

There are many tales about the good things St Nicholas did in his lifetime. In one story he dropped a purse of gold down a chimney to help three girls who were very poor. The purse fell into a stocking hanging up by the fire to dry.

Today we hang up our Christmas stockings in the hope that they will be filled with presents.

What does Father Christmas look like?

This picture by the artist Thomas Nast was published in a magazine in 1881. It was one of the first illustrations to show Father Christmas as a jolly man with a white beard wearing robes trimmed with fur.

Rudolf the red-nosed reindeer

Rudolph and eight other reindeer are said to pull Father Christmas's sleigh as he delivers gifts on the night before Christmas. The reindeer names are:

Dasher Dancer Prancer Vixen Comet Cupid Donner Blitzen ... and Rudolph

Dear Father Christmas...

Lots of children write to Father Christmas each year to tell him what presents they would like for Christmas.

You can write to him at this address:

Father Christmas
Santa's Grotto
Reindeer Land
SAN TA1

Make your own wrapping paper

It is fun to make paper to wrap up presents. Here is a very simple way to do it.

You will need:
* felt-tip pen
* washing-up sponge
* pair of scissors
* poster paints
* plate
* scrap paper
* large sheets of plain paper

Instructions

1 Use the felt-tip pen to draw a simple Christmas shape onto the sponge. A star, a heart, or a Christmas tree all work well.

Cut out the shape.

2 Squeeze a blob of paint onto the plate.

Dab the sponge shape into the paint. Make sure all the shape is covered.

3 Make some prints on the scrap paper to remove any extra paint.

4 Now print the shape all over the large sheet of paper. Then leave it to dry.

5 To add another shape or colour to the wrapping paper design, cut out a second shape from the sponge and repeat the process with a different colour.

Make a chocolate Yule log

This yummy chocolate log is decorated to look like a real **Yule** log in a snowy wood.

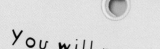

You will need:
* 100g butter
* 150g icing sugar
* 55g cocoa powder
* chocolate Swiss roll
* extra cocoa powder and icing sugar for decoration
* mixing bowl
* large spoon
* knife
* plate

Instructions

1 Beat the butter in a mixing bowl until smooth and then gradually beat in the icing sugar and cocoa powder to make butter cream.

2 Cut off one end of the Swiss roll at an angle. On a plate put the end alongside the Swiss roll to look like a branch.

22

3 Cover all of the Swiss roll with the butter cream. With a fork, make marks in the butter cream to make it look like tree bark. Dust with cocoa powder.

4 To make your log look like a fallen branch in a snowy wood, decorate it with a **sprig** of holly and scatter it with icing sugar to look like snow.

All about Yule

In some countries, people dragged a large Yule log home to burn in the fireplace. It was kept alight for all of the twelve days of Christmas.

The three kings

The Christian festival of **Epiphany** is held on 6 January. It celebrates the time when the three kings arrived at the stable to worship Jesus. The names of the kings were Caspar, Melchior and Balthazar.

Twelfth Night

The evening before Epiphany is often called 'Twelfth Night'. This is because the days from 25 December to 5 January are the 'twelve days of Christmas'. In the past, all twelve days were one long holiday. Epiphany marks the end of Christmas.

Celebrating Epiphany

Epiphany is when the Christmas decorations are put away. It can feel a bit sad. But in some parts of the world it is a day of celebration.

Special day

In France people like to eat a special Epiphany cake, which has a toy crown baked inside it.

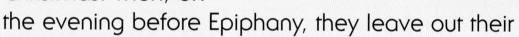

In Spain, Epiphany is called 'The Festival of the Three Magic Kings'. Children have some presents at Christmas. Then, on the evening before Epiphany, they leave out their shoes to be filled up with more presents!

Make a Christmas cracker

Make a Christmas cracker to pull with a friend and see who gets the gift inside!

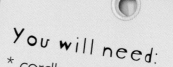

You will need:
* cardboard tube from inside a kitchen roll
* pair of scissors
* bright wrapping paper
* small gift and a joke written on a piece of paper
* sticky tape
* 2 x 30cm pieces of ribbon

Instructions

1 Cut the cardboard tube in half. Cut one of these halves in half again.

2 Lay the paper on the table. Take the larger part of the tube and place it in the middle. Place the joke and the small gift inside. Put the smaller tubes at either end, leaving a narrow space between the tubes.

3 Roll the wrapping paper round the tubes and use a small piece of tape to hold it together. Tie in-between the tubes with the ribbon.

4 Remove the two small tubes from the ends.

The first crackers

A London pastry cook called Tom Smith invented Christmas crackers in Victorian times. The design was based on French sweets that were wrapped in colourful twists of paper. It was Tom who added tiny explosions to give each cracker a 'bang' as it was pulled.

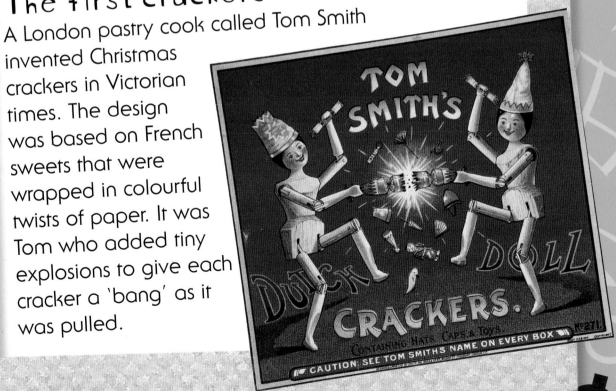

TOM SMITH'S
DUTCH DOLL
CRACKERS.
CONTAINING HATS, CAPS & TOYS.
CAUTION: SEE TOM SMITHS NAME ON EVERY BOX

Make a Christmas muffin jar

This is a tasty present for anyone who loves to cook their own muffins!

You will need:
* clean clear glass jar with a tight-fitting lid
* dessertspoon
* 2tsp baking powder
* 250g self-raising flour
* 175g soft brown sugar
* 25g cocoa powder
* 35g milk chocolate chips
* 45g white chocolate chips
* piece of card 6cm x 8cm
* felt-tip pen
* wooden spoon
* hole punch and ribbon

Instructions

1 Mix the baking powder with the self-raising flour. Spoon the mixture into the jar. Press it down with the spoon.

2 Put the soft brown sugar on top of the flour mixture. Press it down with the spoon.

3 Put the cocoa powder on top of the sugar. Press it down with the spoon.

4 Mix the chocolate chips together. Put them on top of the cocoa powder. Put on the lid.

5 Write the muffin recipe on the piece of card.

Turn the card over. Write 'Chocolate chip muffin mix' on the card.

6 Use the hole punch to make a hole in the top of the card. Thread the ribbon through the hole. Tie on the wooden spoon.

Chocolate chip muffin recipe

Tip the contents of this jar into a large mixing bowl.

Add 175ml milk, 2 large eggs (beaten), 100ml sunflower oil and 1-2tsp vanilla extract. Mix well.

Spoon the mixture into muffin cases.

Bake for 20 minutes at 180°c, gas mark 5.

CHOCOLATE CHIP MUFFIN MIX

Glossary

Advent The time before Christmas that begins on the fourth Sunday before Christmas and lasts until Christmas Eve.

congregation A group of people who are gathered together for religious worship.

engaged When two people are engaged, they have promised to marry each other.

Epiphany A Christian celebration on 6 January that marks the time when the three kings arrived at the stable to worship Jesus. It is the end of the Christmas period.

frankincense A sticky resin from a tree that has a delicious perfume.

manger A container that is used to hold the feed for animals.

Mass One of the services in the Christian church.

midwinter The middle of winter is the time around 21 December when the days are at their shortest.

myrrh An expensive spice that has a delicious perfume, used for making incense.

priest The person who takes a service in the Christian church.

sprig A stem with leaves or flowers on a plant.

swaddling clothes Narrow strips of cloth that are wrapped around a newborn baby to hold its arms and legs still.

taxes Money that people have to pay to a government, or to the rulers of a country.

Twelfth Night The evening of the twelfth day of Christmas, the night before Epiphany.

Yule An old-fashioned word for Christmas.

Index